6 KEYS TO
PROFESSIONAL HAPPINESS
Creating Balance and Fulfillment in Your Career

By Andre Cooke

ISBN-10: 0996569405
ISBN-13: 978-0-9965694-0-8

Printed in the United States of America

For permission requests, write to the publisher, addressed "Attention: Permissions Coordinator," at the address below.

info@opportunepublishing.com
www.opportunepublishing.com

Disclaimer

Although the author and publisher have made every effort to ensure that the information in this book was correct at press time, the author and publisher do not assume and hereby disclaim any liability to any party for any loss, damage, or disruption caused by errors or omissions, whether such errors or omissions result from negligence, accident, or any other cause.

Table of Contents

PREFACE

It's 8:30 p.m. and it feels like I ran a marathon today!

I woke up at 5:00 a.m., exercised, reviewed my to-do list from yesterday, and merged unfinished items from that list with my new priorities for today. From there my calendar looked like a young child's coloring assignment with numerous colorful meeting placeholders covering my day.

Despite the demands on my time, I feel lucky. Actually, I am extremely lucky to be in my current position. I managed hundreds of people and multimillion-dollar projects by the age of 30. Quite an accomplishment for a kid from LA (Lower Alabama) who never knew what career path he wanted to pursue.

Fortunately for me, I stumbled upon success, but I often ask myself "Am I truly happy with my life?" For some reason success always seemed like maintaining a flexible work schedule, conducting deals over lunch, and being nationally recognized.

Searching for professional happiness prompted me to talk with numerous colleagues, friends, and mere strangers to better define what professional happiness means. Can professional happiness be achieved in large corporations, or is it something realized by entrepreneurs? I single out this group because entrepreneurs tend to use their inner passion as the driver of their success.

I always assumed professional fulfillment would hinge upon my financial gains, on the large number of people I managed, or even worse on my professional title. I know, it is so sad but true. Years ago I had no personal understanding of what professional happiness meant outside of these warped perceptions.

Over the course of my career, I have observed common themes that many professionals struggle with, such as:

"Do I make a difference at work?"
"Does my boss value the work I do?"
"Why don't the decision makers listen to me?"
"Am I fulfilled at work?"

I suspect you have had similar introspective questions during your morning or afternoon commute. Many professionals struggle with these basic concepts, as we are ultimately seeking recognition for our contributions and validation for our work.

Most of us tend to falsely measure success by accounting ratios, satisfaction survey results, or promotional increases. My friends, this is no way to live life! I've been down this path and it took guidance from trusted mentors to broaden my perspective of what is truly important in life.

If you could go back to the day you graduated from high school or college and relive your life, would you repeat history or change direction? Most people answer this question unequivocally committing to changing the directions of their lives. Why do so many people wish to change paths? What prevents us from becoming the successful professionals we were destined to be?

Ultimately, life isn't a fairy tale, although we all wish it were. We all want to be AHW—attractive, healthy, and wealthy! While I don't have insight into how to become AHW, I can share my journey to finding happiness, which may be more attainable.

For starters, I had to define what happiness meant to me. My personal definition is at the intersection of freedom and opportunity, but without a roadmap it took some time for me to find it. I admit it's quite difficult to quantify happiness considering that its meaning changes periodically.

For me, I chose to rely on my career in corporate America as my vehicle to professional happiness. This is partially due to being risk averse, but ultimately I love my company and feel fortunate to work with my colleagues.

However, those attributes alone have not made me happy. Over the past two years, I have found six things that make me feel balanced and fulfilled. Hopefully, you can apply these concepts to your life and find your professional happiness.

EXPLORE YOUR INTERESTS

Typically, when you see people who have both success and happiness, they work in areas that fuel their passions. Having passion for the work you do helps provide the longevity needed to sustain a long-lasting career. Although this concept seems rather simple, there are some hidden risks.

Take my dentist Craig for example. He oversees a successful dental practice with fifteen employees. On the surface, Craig has everything imaginable, but he is unhappy with the direction of his life.

He has mentioned on numerous occasions, "It was not supposed to be like this. I imagined myself having more balance with work and my family. However, I work excessively and my family accepts the fact that I am rarely around. They have been conditioned to make excuses for me and to not criticize my absences from major family events."

Although Craig dreamed of being a successful dentist, he never anticipated the sacrifices he would make to reach his dream. Craig was so fixated on being an independent dentist that he overlooked the business aspects of owning a dental practice. He didn't think about marketing, payroll, taxes, and other core business functions. Being responsible for these tasks in addition to general dentistry has caused Craig to dread going to the office daily.

Most people are on the other side of the spectrum; they ended up in their careers by chance and find it more challenging to create the high level of passion needed to sustain their work. Exploring your interests is difficult if they fall outside of your current career. However, part of your success was created by your ability to excel in certain aspects of your job. Find those areas that align with your core strengths and exploit them.

For instance, I have a friend, Lisa, who is a middle manager for a major corporation. She hates dealing with employee personnel issues and quarterly sales quotas. However, Lisa thrives at recruiting and building leadership-preparedness programs.

Although dealing with employee personnel issues and quarterly sales quotas remain key parts of her responsibilities, she has strengthened her professional brand by creating high-potential development programs. Lisa's passion has differentiated her from peers and provided her a broader platform to showcase her abilities.

While working through all the pros and cons of her job, Lisa has been successful in changing how she feels about work and has been validated by the results she achieved via exploring her passion.

There are times when exploring your interests leads you to a different career path, and other times when finding outside interests provides balance for you personally and professionally.

Two years ago I was faced with a personal quandary. I was happy with my career and overall quality of life but still felt like something important was missing. Despite juggling many competing priorities, I was seeking for ways to make a broader impact with my life.

Like a flash of lightning, it hit me! I'm a blessed individual and wasn't finding time to help others around me grow. Every Saturday morning I was lying in bed watching my weekend dose of sports and classic '80s television shows. I could take a few hours away from this weekly routine and commit to doing something more productive. I pledged to volunteer with two organizations that resonated with me. In this case, exploring my personal interests helped balance me both personally and professionally.

Realizing there is a need to change is the first step to finding professional happiness, but identifying what areas to change is more important. You have to be brutally honest with yourself and solicit feedback from others around you.

Once you identify areas to change, you must set measurable goals for yourself. It's very difficult to change behaviors without measuring your progress; without measurement you may be somewhat delusional about your perceived change. Remember, change doesn't happen overnight, but you have the power to create and sustain change.

Find passion in your current job, and if it doesn't exist, create an environment that increases your opportunity to thrive and enjoy your work. If you're like Craig and currently in a career path of which you had always dreamed, reinvent your passion. If you stumbled into your career and currently lack motivation, identify the facets of your job that you love and exploit them.

~Remember, we all have to be the catalysts for our personal change.~

DON'T CHASE THE MONEY

"Money can be a source of happiness and also a source of sadness." I suspect you have heard this a few times in your life, yet we all can't quite seem to get enough money. Better yet, the more money you make, the more you need to affirm your existence in this world.

I recall my first job out of college when I was making $36,000 a year and feeling like I was on top of the world! Every weekend I explored my new city with family and friends. As I accounted for my expenses on Monday mornings, I typically spent $100 and I would say to myself, "I have to stay at home and spend less money next weekend!"

Flash forward several years: I spend that same $100 on unplanned Tuesday night dinners with coworkers or friends. I was once conscious about budgeting for that amount, and now it shows up in the spontaneous-expense category. Why the change in my saving pattern?

Unfortunately, I fell into a trap that so many others do: my spending and personal expectations gradually increased over the years with my annual raises. I know, I read the books and was warned to avoid this reckless behavior, but I'm human. I suspect I'm not the only one who has given into worldly indulgences and temptation.

For starters, we live in a society that touts wealth and power as necessary ingredients to a happy life. Wealth is thus admired and is the driving factor behind so many young men and women attending college right now. In fact, capitalism is at the heart of the American dream.

Most of us dream of owning fine homes, sleek cars, and taking elaborate vacations around the world. What's wrong with having these desires? I'm glad you asked the question. There is nothing wrong with wanting wealth. I want it just as much as you do! However, when financial gain is the only driver for success, there are inherent problems with maintaining professional happiness.

Most people don't make a fortune by working forty-hour workweeks. Most high-net-worth individuals attained their wealth by leveraging their strong work ethic, passion, vision, and dedication to their crafts. Sometimes important things like nurturing family relationships become secondary in our personal quest to obtain professional success.

We all see this. Remember Craig from earlier in this book; his wife and kids reap the rewards of his success while he has a great deal of stress and is unable to fully enjoy his financial gains. He continues down his current path because his family depends on him to maintain their lifestyle.

There are few things worse than having a career that pays well, but the thought of going to work makes you ill. Take a stroll down memory lane with me. I can vividly recall feeling ill when I smelled that unforgettable school smell—the thought alone right now makes me feel nauseated! Well, I recently had a friend make that reference to me.

Katie and I attended college together and stayed in contact over the years. To those around her, it appears that she is on top of the world. She has the perfect family, a desirable role in her company, and great future potential. Those closely connected to Katie would be shocked to know she is miserable due to the pressures she's facing at work.

Why does she stay with her current employer? Katie and her husband have a mortgage, private school tuition for two kids, car notes, student loans, etc. They acquired things in life that are commensurate with their combined salaries and now it's difficult to leave it all behind.

Even worse, I recently learned of health challenges that Katie is facing. In addition to being unhappy, she's having heart problems and stress-induced panic attacks. Sadly, her personal challenges are occurring as her organization is preparing to merge with a competitor and Katie is not sure if she will still be employed next year.

Unhappiness has a way of showing up in several aspects of our lives: there is the thick tension at home between you and your spouse that exists only in your head, the accelerated aging and weight gain you experienced, and the depression that shows more outwardly than you realize.

As humans, we have the innate ability to recognize the distress in one another, but often we lack the emotional intelligence to address this in real-time.

I suggest you identify things that you enjoy and wrap your career path around those hobbies and interests. For instance, developing and nurturing relationships with people is something that I genuinely enjoy and this aligns with my current leadership role.

I once heard someone say, "You can chase the money, or let the money chase you." What a profound statement! When you are happy with the work you do, you do a better job. Ultimately, your products or services are in higher demand and your income grows due to your heightened engagement and enthusiasm.

Identify the type of life that you want for yourself and build your career around that dream. It may not always be easy, but your journey will ultimately be filled with fewer bruises and less heartache than the journey of those who have gone down the alternative path.

The speed of life seems to be faster than the speed of light these days. There is time only to think about your short-term wants and not nearly enough time to plan for your long-term needs. Make time! You only get one shot at life and you deserve happiness.

~Money will come and go, but happiness
and peace lasts an eternity.~

SET REALISTIC GOALS

Like you, I would also love to be a multimillionaire this year with no signs of the incoming cash flow slowing down. Unfortunately for me, that is unlikely to happen but instead remains a lofty goal.

One of the biggest barriers to professional success is unrealistic personal expectations. As a result of our sincerely innocent attempts to be high achievers, we sometimes overlook obvious challenges. I believe in chasing your dreams, but always temper dreams with an element of reality. Don't be so foolish as to overlook obvious challenges, and don't be afraid to address those issues head-on.

I recently mentored a young man who mentioned that he wanted to be an executive of his company in five years. This was a great goal, but was it attainable? After researching career paths for executive leaders in his organization, we learned that it took the average executive twenty years to obtain his or her position.

The reality is my mentee is currently in an

entry-level role and needs time to learn key business functions. There are also many talented employees in the company's leadership pipeline. While I don't enjoy crushing anyone's goal, I do find great joy in reshaping goals that are realistic and achievable.

We identified my mentee's true aspirations for the next five years of his career: broader responsibility in his organization, increased yearly pay, and opportunities to heighten his visibility. More importantly, we outlined the things he needed to do to achieve these desired outcomes. He agreed to continue his education, serve as a resource to others, seek opportunities to expand his influence on key projects, and pursue internal networking. If he follows through with the items listed that he controls, he will undoubtedly secure the increased responsibility, pay, and notoriety that he is currently seeking with his company.

My mentee is very ambitious and is committed to doing the necessary things to advance at his company. There are others who have the skills needed to advance in their current field but continually hit brick walls when promotional opportunities arise. Some people know all the rules of the game but simply choose to ignore them.

For example, the company I work for values professionals who deepen their understanding of our business and seek industry certifications. Many people I speak with who have leadership potential say, "I understand the importance of obtaining certifications, but I don't have time right now. Things are hectic balancing my kids, spouse, and other commitments. However, I'm the most talented person in my department. Why don't they promote me on my past performance alone?"

I hear these comments often, and without fail it baffles me every time. I term this thought process "exception thinking." Even though these individuals know what it takes to advance, they are looking for exceptions because they think they are special. People who demonstrate exception thinking fail to realize that the only person holding them back from greater opportunities is the complacent person residing inside of them.

Oftentimes our goals are too broad, which prevents us from determining the appropriateness or intent of the goal. This precludes us from establishing progress checkpoints along our journey. Goals must stretch you to do more than you would have without the goals, but they must also be attainable. For instance, if you make $50,000 yearly after taxes, it may be unrealistic for you to save $35,000 a year due to expenses for your home, food, student loan repayments, etc. However, saving $15,000 a year may be more attainable.

From my experiences, when you form the habit or underlying behavior to help you reach your goal, it becomes your routine. Your newly formed habit becomes more difficult to break without serious consideration. Think about the first time you saved a significant amount of money—it was likely euphoric. If you're like me, you checked your bank account a few times to ensure you accomplished your goal, and you sought ways to reduce your spending and save even more money.

So how does this concept relate to your professional happiness? Too often, we set unrealistic goals to reach peaks outside of our range. Whether you work in an organization or you are an entrepreneur, you must push yourself, but not to the point of obsession or your goal will become unhealthy.

I have seen this happen too many times in my career. People with unrealistic expectations attempt to prove everyone wrong and ultimately fizzle out over time. Balance in your goal setting is key here.

When it comes to setting realistic goals, three concepts come to mind:

1. Plan
2. Benchmark
3. Celebrate

Planning appears to be the most obvious of the three concepts. We have all heard the saying, "If you don't have a plan, you are planning to fail." Yes, I know this is cliché but it is so true. In terms of your professional happiness, planning will force you to be introspective and think about how you want to be defined. Do you want to be an executive leader in the organization, or the top sales leader in your district? Maybe you are content being the valued analyst who finds time to coach and volunteer on the weekend?

If you plan for it, you can have it all. Set manageable goals for yourself and others. Colleagues and business partners have to know what's acceptable, and you ultimately establish those boundaries. Set clear dividers between work and family to be your very best in both areas.

It's critical to set goals and more important to benchmark your progress along the way. Like creating a plan, this is very elementary and often overlooked. For those of you with kids, progress reports are key indicators that show how your kids are progressing in school.

Progress reports show insight of what to expect with final grades, while providing an opportunity to adjust. As you plan your career, personal life, and ultimate happiness, you must use progress reports for similar purposes.

Why is it so important to have benchmarks and check progress? Life happens! New relationships, illness, marriage, divorce, unexpected expenses, and the interruptions continue to infinity. Benchmarking doesn't prevent these life events from occurring; rather it ensures a level of accountability so that you can reach your long-term goals despite the unplanned events. Commitment and determination are needed to attain your strategic goals.

Lastly, you have to find time to celebrate your successes. It's easy to dwell in a pessimistic world, but this mindset doesn't benefit you. Life will throw obstacles your way; turn these negative situations into positive situations and celebrate how you responded to the adversity.

Life wasn't meant to be a fairytale. Your internal strength was built by the way you overcame your toughest personal challenges.

~Embrace challenges; grow and apply lessons learned to future successes.~

BELIEVE

"I would be so much farther ahead if only I had received that promotion last year."
"Why didn't I choose a different major in college?"
"There is simply not enough time in my life to go back to school right now."

We all tend to fill our heads with self-doubt, which masks our deep-rooted fears related to success. I realize this may sound odd at first, but think about it for a moment. The only thing preventing you from accomplishing any goal or dream is you. Sure, there are natural obstacles in life, but successful individuals are pretty good at overcoming barriers and accomplishing their dreams against all odds.

For instance, I know a mother who raised four kids and found herself in the empty-nester stage of life. This was very difficult, as her life had been full of preparing meals, doing laundry, and attending school and athletic activities. However, she had always dreamed of becoming a registered nurse and helping others.

Well, as you can imagine her friends and family laughed at the idea of her going to college while in her 50s! Well she decided to pursue her dream and enrolled in nursing school. Sure, she didn't quite fit in with her classmates, and she wasn't as tech-savvy as the other students, but she is now a thriving registered nurse!

Was it easy? She would scream at the top of her voice "no!" Along the way, she learned that coffee was her friend during late-night study sessions. There were many times she felt inferior to younger, sharper classmates, but she didn't waver from her goal. Ultimately, belief in herself and stubbornness to prove naysayers wrong fueled her accomplishment.

Many of us have the same drive she displayed to accomplish her educational and career pursuits, but we lack the discipline to commit during the tough times. It's easy to accomplish goals that require minimal effort. When you truly make up your mind to tackle a difficult task, you agree to push when it hurts, to stay the course when the waters get choppy, and to sometimes travel your journey alone.

You can do it; I believe you can! Sure, there will be peaks and valleys, but keep pressing forward. You are destined for success and have been provided the tools necessary to reach the finish line. You must believe in yourself, have faith, and continue to strive toward your goal.

I realize this encouragement may seem like a high-school cheerleader pumping up the football team, and it should. We all need more cheerleaders in our lives. We need to surround ourselves with people who recognize our potential, don't allow us to settle for mediocrity, and push us forward.

How many times have you watched a sporting event where everyone knew who the winner should have been based on statistics, talent levels, and past performances, only to see David defeat Goliath? It happens all the time, and it's a result of believing and being outwardly optimistic.

One of my best friends in life finds ways to encourage me when I'm crawling in despair and pushes me when I feel like I've conquered the world. I'm never allowed to be content with the status quo. There is always a push to dream bigger and accomplish more.

Find that person in your life and use him or her as your accountability partner. There may be times when your personal relationship with your accountability partner suffers, but from experience, my personal growth has been immeasurable.

Belief and happiness are closely related in my world because they are interdependent. In order for you to achieve happiness, you have to take a leap of faith and believe. Be prepared to roll up your sleeves and work outside of your comfort zone. You may become sleep deprived during the process, or go without weekly indulgences; however, sacrificing is okay and it makes the final reward so much sweeter.

There are also times in life when you simply have to claim your destiny. When you believe it and work hard, you will achieve it. I have an equation on my whiteboard at home that reads: Dreams + Hard Work + Persistence = Professional Happiness. I truly believe in this concept. It takes all parts on the left side of the equation to achieve the right side.

Believe in yourself when no one else around you believes. Know you can overcome any stumbling block or hurdle life brings your way. When times get tough, and they will, say out loud "I believe!" You will be amazed at what you can accomplish via sheer determination.

Doors are meant to open and close. In life, when a door seems impossible to open, regroup and try harder to open the door, or look for someone to assist you. Sometimes it simply takes a different approach to open the door to your dreams.

~Don't allow anyone to take away your dream or adversely impact your ability to achieve greatness.~

HARD WORK PAYS OFF

Speaking of my equation to achieve Professional Happiness referenced in the prior chapter, hard work is a necessary ingredient in the recipe for happiness. This concept can be somewhat ambiguous, as its meaning tends to change based on what our immediate goal is.

Conceptually, the hard work needed to finish medical school is vastly different from the hard work needed to dig a ditch; yet in some twisted sense, the definition remains the same for both tasks.

There is often discussion about which is more taxing; manual or mental labor. I have done both and believe they are equally challenging. With that being said, they are also both essential to shaping your brand.

I recently had a chance to meet with a professional dancer on Broadway. On the surface, she lives a glamorous life that anyone would envy. She makes a nice living doing something that she is passionate about, and enjoys prestigious fringe benefits that enable her to explore the many treasures of the world.

While chatting about her current achievements, she quickly corrected me and said her success was not without sacrifice. Through descriptive storytelling I saw a girl who worked tirelessly to master her craft.

I was told of a young girl who overcame numerous injuries to advance her dance career. I was introduced to a young adult who was practically homeless because casting directors couldn't see her potential in a sea of dancers. She did not allow any of these challenges to stop her; she continued to work hard, refined her dance techniques, and eventually found success.

No matter how you try to avoid it, there is no substitute for old-fashioned hard work. Many of us would like to skip this part of the equation and advance to happiness. However, for most of us this is impossible, which is why we return to work after each long day.

Over my life, I have seen the role that hard work has had in shaping me into the person I am today. Also, I have learned to embrace difficult situations as opportunities. For every area of my life in which I had to roll up my sleeves and work harder, there was a lesson learned that was far greater and more valuable than the work I did.

Some lessons allowed me to avoid catastrophic mistakes in my life, while others taught me the importance of going through things in a sequential manner to perfect the end product. Other lessons taught me the importance of doing the right thing even when it was the most difficult thing to do.

As a technologically advanced society, we have strayed somewhat from teaching and demonstrating what a strong work ethic looks like. Advertisers and inventors see this and develop campaigns and products to target our desire for easy substitutes of hard work and commitment. We see it everyday. There are tons of infomercials marketing quick-weight-loss products, get-rich-quick investments, and the list goes on and on.

Sure, gimmicky products and advertisements are enticing; and you sometimes see temporary gains, but do they last? I have tried many shortcuts in my life, only to find myself further away from my original goals.

Hard work is important for your professional

happiness because it is necessary in order to fully appreciate the benefits of your success.

We sometimes try to take the easiest route toward happiness, only to find that the destination wasn't as golden as it appeared in our dreams. Having fallen into this trap a few times in my life, I have learned that there is no shortcut to happiness.

Too often we want to avoid hard work like the plague, when really it's what we need. Look back over your life and think about the things you were given versus the things you earned. You likely place a higher value on things you earned, saved for, or invested a tremendous amount of sweat equity into.

When you work hard to achieve a goal, you have a better understanding of its overall value and a greater appreciation for the accomplishment. This reinforces the idea that it's okay to work hard, and you are better served for going through the process. Don't shortcut this area, as it cheapens your final destination.

To achieve goals you have to commit for the long haul. Combining belief and hard work is a blueprint for accomplishing your biggest dreams.

It's equally important that you remember to invest in yourself. Oftentimes, we are willing to invest in everything except ourselves. You are the most important person in your life. The more you put into yourself, the more you can give to those around you.

Find time to build your skills and expand your influence. Promote your brand proudly. It is a byproduct of your hard work. Understand your value. Celebrate both the work put into becoming the person you are today and your plans for the future.

~Anything in life worth having is worth the hard work.~

INTEGRITY GOES A LONG WAY

It's difficult to go through life without purpose, yet so many people find themselves aimlessly searching for direction.

The world is full of distractions and negative influences, and this bad energy is not absent from the work environment. Despite the constant struggle between good and bad, you and I must remain steadfast in our pursuit of always doing the right things.

I have a neighbor who is currently completing a virtual MBA program while working full-time as an accountant. He recently shared how a friend tempted him to shortchange his educational experience by cheating on a final exam. It was a technology course that required students to complete a virtual project to pass the course. Prior students had mapped out the entire exercise and could change variables that the professor would check to determine whether the final project was worthy of a passing grade. Although my neighbor is not very tech-savvy and could have benefited from cheating, he decided the reward didn't outweigh the risk of getting caught and expelled from the university.

My neighbor faced a basic dilemma that we have all seen countless times in our lives: whether or not to act ethically. Preparation for these types of situations started when we were young.

Our parents provided moral framework by defining what is right versus what is wrong; more importantly, they established consequences to influence our decision-making. My neighbor could have easily spent a few dollars and obtained a completed copy of his final project, but it wasn't the right thing to do and he declined the offer.

In the pursuit of happiness, we all face moral dilemmas that may appear to accelerate our journey to increased wealth, power, or happiness. Hopefully, when you are faced with these situations you innately respond ethically. This is critical when building and representing your personal brand.

Assumptions, opinions, and perceptions are formed daily about who we are as individuals and the threshold of our moral boundaries.

Albeit sometimes unfounded, perception impacts promotions and the level of responsibility others are willing to bestow on us as an official representative of their company or business interests.

Remain true to your core when tested, even when it appears to be to your detriment. For starters, you maintain internal peace knowing that you followed your heart and did the right thing when presented with a dilemma. Also, people around you notice and admire your commitment to standing up for what you believe in. Lastly, you avoid any negative consequences for making decisions that go against your morals.

Being trustworthy is fundamental in the business world, and we all need people around us who exhibit this trait. Although some leaders operate in cultures in which backstabbing and public shame are the norms, those individuals rarely have professional longevity. Successful people are balanced and have a history of exhibiting ethically strong decision-making skills.

Decisions are typically better when diversity of thought is embraced. Although groups of decision makers tend to see things from a broader lens than a single individual, there are times when the lone holdout has the right answer.

Sometimes people displaying groupthink will attempt to alter your core or suggest that you are somewhat off base with your analysis of a particular situation. Remember your ability to decipher wrong from right stems from your experiences and has been tested countless times during your life. There may be smarter or more experienced people in the group, but integrity is an area where your instincts will help you make the right decision.

I'm reminded of a story where there was a product in high demand, and it was the company's goal to find ways to increase manufacturing of the product. Along the way, defects were noticed and could have been easily fixed, but this would have tainted consumer image and stalled production.

The decision was made to forge ahead without addressing the issue noticed by factory workers. Well, over time the defects became very obvious to consumers and a class action lawsuit was filed because the company marketed defective products.

Today this company no longer manufactures products. If the executive leadership team could go back and alter their decision, would they? I think so. Had the company made the needed changes to the product and announced improvements, consumer confidence may have taken a dip. But in reality, loyal customers would have returned if the products were better. Choosing to conceal problems made customers question the integrity of the company, and support for the company and its products was lost.

We must all be aware that there are consequences for our actions, whether right or wrong. Knowing this should play a critical role in how we make decisions.

The moral of this story is to be true to who you are and what you believe in. It's not always easy to make decisions with integrity, but it's the only thing to do, and integrity prevails.

~Do the right thing, even when it's difficult.~

CONCLUSION

As you are well aware, professional happiness is difficult to define due to its nebulous meaning. However, that doesn't prevent us from chasing happiness. In fact we should seek happiness in every aspect of our lives, but particularly in our professional existences.

As an adult, how you feel about life is often predicated on how you feel about your career. In order to maintain a healthy perspective on the world, you need to find enjoyment and fulfillment in your professional life.

In a world with many competing priorities, we tend to overlook the importance people have in our life. We owe so much to those who influenced, provided guidance, or simply served as listening ears. The more we invest in meaningful relationships, the more enriched our lives become. Make it a priority to connect often with those who fuel you, and pay forward this selfless act. Remember, sometimes your network influences your net worth.

Do things that genuinely make you happy. If you are in a situation in which you are unable to be genuinely happy, change it. As opposed to becoming toxic to others, serve as an inspirational example of someone who sought improvement of his or her situation.

As with most things in life, balance is key. Be centered on your goals and reality. Realize that too much of a good thing can be harmful. Your legacy should be defined by doing great things personally and professionally. You can accomplish your dreams and enjoy life simultaneously.

Like Craig from earlier in the book, explore career options in which you have genuine interest and passion. While realizing your goals, you may find some aspects undesirable. Find ways to reshape these areas, or surround yourself with business partners who fill the gaps. Also, don't forget about Lisa who exploited the areas of her current job at which she excels.

Believe in yourself and know that failure is not an option. Your destiny is yours to claim, should you choose. Accept responsibility for your past, but don't dwell on your mistakes. Apply lessons learned to your future, which demonstrates your growth.

Be strategic about creating happiness in both your personal and professional lives. Be truthful with yourself about your needs and wants. Remember that you ultimately control the quality of life you and your family enjoy.

As you find professional happiness and success, remain humble. Don't forget those noble attributes that made you successful, and display them proudly. Too often people become victims of their own success; don't allow this to happen to you.

Be authentic in your personal and professional relationships. People need to see the real you at all times. Never waver from your moral core and those around you will respect this quality.

The journey to professional happiness will be long with many twists and turns, but find enjoyment in the process. Celebrate people, failures, achievements, and most importantly you. When you decide to pursue happiness, you have left your comfort zone and venture into the unknown. Regardless of where you ultimately land, follow your heart and chase your dreams; this is worth celebrating!

~Despite the ups and downs, always be proud of the person you are.~

Call to Press

If you are interested in booking this author for readings or other events, please use the contact information below.

Email:
6keystoprofessionalhappiness@gmail.com

Website:
www.6keystohappiness.com

Facebook:
https://www.facebook.com/pages/6-Keys-To-Professional-Happiness/852312291526587

Instagram:
https://instagram.com/6keystoprofessionalhappiness/

Twitter:
https://twitter.com/6keys2happiness